DIVINE THREADS

A SOUL UNFOLDING

Golden Heart

I am the weaver and the thread. Each word is
a return to my soul. I surrender to truth, to
love , to legacy —
Knowing that what flows through me is
Divine.

Table of Contents

Opening Prayer

May these words be a doorway.
May they remind you of the versions of yourself
you've outgrown, honored, healed, and reclaimed.

May every page meet you where you are
and guide you gently to where your spirit is rising.

I pray that clarity finds you.
I pray that peace holds you.
I pray that courage follows you
into every chapter you're meant to live next.

To the ones becoming—
may you remember your power.
To the ones healing—
may you remember your softness.
To the ones rising—
may you remember your wings.

Ase'.

✦ Why I Wrote This Book

I wrote this book for anyone standing at the edge of their own becoming —
the woman shedding old versions of herself,
the man searching for his voice again,
the soul learning to rise after seasons that tried to dim their light.

These pages were born from my own healing,
from moments where I had to choose myself
even when it scared me,
even when it stretched me,
even when it broke me open
just enough for the light to get in.

I wrote this for the person who is tired of shrinking.
For the heart learning softness again after surviving too much.
For the spirit who knows they're called to more
but isn't sure how to take the first step.
For anyone who has been unmade by life
and is now piecing themselves back together
with intention, grace, and God.

This book is a witness.
A mirror.
A offering.
A reminder that you are not alone
in your unraveling or your rising.

These words came through me
so they could live in you —
to soothe, to awaken,
to affirm the truth you've always carried:

You are allowed to evolve.
You are allowed to outgrow what wounded you.
You are allowed to be both soft and strong.
And you are allowed to become someone
your past self would be proud of.

If this book finds you in a moment of transition,
may it guide you gently home
to the most honest, unbound version of yourself.

Ase'.
— Cece Hayes

SECTION I - UNBOUND

"When I learned what didn't belong to me anymore."
Section Intro Draft:
These are the poems born in the breaking.
The unlearning.
The slow, aching release of everything I held onto out of survival, duty, or fear.
This is the place where I faced the version of myself who stayed too long, loved too hard, carried too much, and forgot her own reflection trying to keep others whole.
Here is where I loosened the knots—
the vows I outgrew, the wounds I normalized, the silence I swallowed, the dreams I buried to make room for someone else's comfort.
In these pages, I became unbound.
Untied.
Unhidden.
This is where I learned to walk away not out of anger, but out of awakening.
Not because I stopped loving,
but because I finally remembered the woman I was born to become.

UNBOUND — The Release

This is where the unraveling begins.
Where silence breaks, truth surfaces,
and the body remembers what it has
been carrying.
These poems are not gentle — they are
honest.
They loosen what was bound too tightly
and name what could no longer stay.

This is not bitterness.
This is freedom speaking for the first
time.

Held Hostage

I was not bound by chains—
but by memory.
By the echo of who I used to be
reaching for me in moments of doubt.

I stayed loyal to pain
because it was familiar.
I called it patience.
I called it love.
I called it healing
before I was healed.

I let the past rent space in my body,
paced the halls of my nervous system,
whispered lies that sounded like truth:
"This is as good as it gets."

But today—
I reclaim my breath.
I loosen the grip of old versions
that only knew how to survive.

I forgive the woman
who didn't know how to leave yet.
I bless the girl
who stayed too long.

I am no longer negotiating with ghosts.
I am no longer imprisoned by history.

The door was never locked.

I was just afraid
of who I'd be
once I walked free.

✦ What I Never Said the Last Time You Left

(UNBOUND)
I swallowed so many words
trying to keep the peace
that I forgot what my own voice sounded like.

Every time you left,
I stayed quiet—
thinking silence would save us,
thinking softness would fix you,
thinking loyalty meant losing pieces of myself
to prove I was worth coming back to.

What I never said is this:

I was tired.
Tired of shrinking.
Tired of pretending.
Tired of holding a love
that never learned how to hold me back.

You mistook my patience for permission.
My forgiveness for forgetting.
My softness for surrender.

But the truth is—
every goodbye you gave me
became a hello to myself.

I didn't lose you.
I found me.

So here's what I never said
when you walked out the last time:

Leaving hurt,
but staying would've killed me.
And I chose my life.

I chose my voice.
I chose my freedom.
I chose the woman who was buried beneath the compromise.
I chose the future I deserved
over the past I survived.

And now?
I don't wait at doors that close themselves.
I don't beg for love that forgets my name.
I don't bargain with my own becoming.

What I never said the last time you left
is that I finally understood—

You were never my ending.
Just the lesson I needed
to rise.

“My Body Doesn’t Flinch Anymore”

for the woman whose nervous system has been rewired by love

There was a time
when footsteps near my door
made me shrink.

A time when tone
meant danger,
not depth.

When a compliment
felt like bait.
And softness
felt like a setup
for pain.

But not anymore.

My body knows now
how to rest in safety.
Not survival.
Not suspense.

I don't hold my breath
when I'm being loved.
I don't prepare
for the crash
when something feels too good.

Because now—
good can stay.

Now—
gentle is real.
Not just a pause before the storm.

I've become the kind of woman
whose body believes her love story
isn't going to hurt her.

And that's not a fairytale.
That's nervous system healing.
That's soul work in the flesh.
That's God moving through my spine.

I don’t flinch anymore.
I receive.
I rest.
I rise.
✦ Ase.

Stillness Was the Shift”

There was a time when rushing felt like progress.
When being busy meant being worthy.
When silence felt like failure
and stillness, like surrender.

But something sacred happened
the moment the noise was no longer enough.

Stillness became sanctuary.
Softness became strength.
And nothing needed proving.

Now, there is room for breath.
Room for truth to echo across lifetimes.
Room to bloom — not to impress,
but to remember what it means to simply be.

The shift wasn’t loud.
It was a whisper.
But it changed everything.

I honor the stillness that shaped me. I no longer need the noise.

Peace Is My Favorite Revenge

I used to think I had to clap back
to prove I wasn't broken.

Now I know—
my calm is louder
than anything they could ever say.

Peace became my sharpest edge.
Not because it hurts,
but because it confuses
the ones who expected me to bleed.

I don't match energy anymore.
I protect mine.
I don't scream to be understood—
I rest, I rise,
I move like a woman who remembers
her power doesn't need permission.

Because now?
I don't want revenge.
I want nothing where chaos once lived.

Let them wonder how I stayed soft and still won."

★

She Was Patient, But Not Passive

She waited,
but not with folded hands or closed
heart.
She waited like seeds beneath the soil—
gathering, stretching,
trusting spring would remember her.
She didn't chase love.
She called it in with stillness, with
standards, with softness
that did not apologize for its strength.
She was patient, but not passive — each
delay, each silence, each almost
became a verse in her becoming.
She trusted the Divine more than her
doubt.
And when it arrived— real, rooted,
radiant — she didn't question the timing.
She had already become
the kind of woman worth the wait.

I do not chase. I attract.
What belongs to me arrives with ease,
because I have already become it.

+ She No Longer Had to Prove It (UNBOUND)

She used to explain herself to be
accepted—
translate her softness
into language that didn't fit her tongue.
She used to shrink to be loved, to be
understood, to avoid being told she was
"too much" for how deeply she felt.
Now?
She says less.
She moves with knowing.
Her energy speaks louder than her old
need to convince.
She no longer tries to fit inside the
rooms or stories or expectations
that never had space for her truth.

My energy is explanation enough.
I no longer prove—I simply exist in
truth

*

Soft, But Not Silent

She is the quiet storm.
The candle that lights without burning.
The truth you feel
even when she says nothing.

They mistook her softness for surrender.
But she was never weak—
just wise enough to know
that real power doesn't have to raise its voice.

She speaks in presence.
She moves in purpose.
She chooses peace
but carries thunder in her chest
for the moments that require it.

My softness is sacred.
My boundaries are holy.
And my silence is never submission—it's command."

★

✦ What I Refuse to Carry Forward

I release the urge
to explain my worth
to people committed
to misunderstanding me.

I refuse to carry guilt
for outgrowing rooms
that only loved me
when I stayed small.

I leave behind the habit
of overextending grace
to those who never learned
how to hold me gently.

What I carry forward
is discernment.
Boundaries.
A nervous system that knows peace
is not something I earn —
it is something I choose.

I am not bitter.
I am free.

And freedom travels light.

🌿 Healing Poem

"What I Released Didn't Leave Me Empty"

I didn't lose anything
by letting go.

What left
wasn't love—
it was weight.

I didn't become colder.
I became clearer.

Some things exit
not as punishment,
but as protection.

And what stayed
was my breath,
my body,
my peace
still intact.

That's how I knew
it was healing
and not abandonment.

★

Unbound

I am no longer tied
to who I had to be
to survive you.

I release the grip of almosts,
the weight of maybes,
the ache of waiting for what never chose me fully.

I untangle my worth
from your uncertainty.
I unhook my heart
from timelines that were never promised.

What once felt like love
was a lesson in remembering myself.

I am unbound now.
Not bitter.
Not broken.
Just free.

And freedom looks like
me choosing me
without apology.

After the Release”

(Bridge Poem)

I didn’t rise all at once.
I rested.

I sat with the quiet
that followed the truth.
I let my nervous system learn
that peace does not mean absence,
and love does not require survival.

There was a moment
where nothing asked me to be strong.
Nothing pulled.
Nothing begged.

Only breath.
Only choice.

This is where I stopped rehearsing my pain
and began listening for my life.

I am not who I was
when I needed to endure.
I am becoming
someone who gets to stay.

✦ The Threshold
(Bridge Poem)

There was a moment
after the breaking
and before the becoming
where nothing asked me to rush.

No one was calling me forward.
No one was pulling me back.
I stood in the quiet
with my truth
still warm in my hands.

This was the space
where old versions loosened their grip
and new ones had not yet spoken.

Not grief.
Not joy.
Just clarity.

I learned here
that release is not an ending —
it's a widening.
A pause where the soul
checks its footing
before stepping into itself again.

I didn't need to explain
who I was becoming.
I didn't need permission
to move differently.

I only needed courage
to stay with myself
long enough
to hear what was true.

This was the threshold —
where survival softened
into choice.
Where instinct turned into intention.
Where love stopped being something I chased
and became something I carried.

I crossed it quietly.
Not because I was unsure —
but because power doesn't always announce itself.

Some transformations
happen so gently
they feel like peace.

SECTION 2- ROOTED-GROUND

"Before I rose, I had to remember what held me."

Section Intro:

These are the poems born from memory, lineage, and the quiet truths beneath my becoming. This is where the soil of my story lives - the roots, the whispers, the women before me, and the version of myself I had to meet before I could grow.

Rooted

I am grounded in who I am.
No longer swayed by absence.
No longer uprooted by longing.

I stand.

✨ The Ground Knows My Name

Before I was chosen,
I was claimed —
by the earth,
by my breath,
by the knowing in my bones.

I do not float anymore.
I stand.

Anchored

Nothing meant for me
will pass me by.

I am steady.
I am ready.

Home Within

I am no longer searching
for safety outside myself.

I have built it
here.

Motherhood

I mother myself
as gently as I mother you.

I teach love
by embodying it.

Motherhood Mantra

I mother myself
so my child inherits freedom.

I choose presence over perfection.
I choose softness without guilt.

What I heal,
she will never have to carry.

Ase'.

★

A Seat at My Table

They weren't just birds.
They were reminders.
Messengers.
Little winged confirmations
that I was exactly where
I was meant to be.

They landed without fear,
as if they had been waiting
to join me.
As if they recognized
the softness in my spirit,
the calm I had fought so hard
to earn.

Their wings fluttered
like small prayers,
their presence a quiet blessing.
And for a moment,
I felt held.
Witnessed.
Chosen by something gentle.

It wasn't the food on the table —
it was the energy.
The openness.
The peace returning home
to my body.

When the birds sat with me,
I remembered that I am guided.
Protected.
Surrounded by signs
that meet me exactly
where I am.

I realized the world speaks
when I slow down.
And sometimes,
it speaks in wings.

Mantra:

I create space for blessings, and the universe always takes a seat beside me.

She Became the Bridge

(Rooted & Rising)

Not the seed,
not the sun,
but the space between
where both decided to trust.

She stood in the middle,
ankles in the mud,
palms stretched toward light
they said she'd never reach.

She was not born bold—
she became it,
each time she chose to stay soft
without shrinking.

When the old world crumbled,
she whispered,
"I will not go with it."
And meant it.

She didn't bloom for applause.
She bloomed for breath.
For her daughter.
For the ones who came before
and the ones still afraid.

She became the bridge
between the version who doubted
and the one who arrived.

Mantra:
I am the bridge. I am the root. I am the answered prayer in bloom. 🌱

The Bloom Beyond the Bridge

(Rooted & Rising section)

There was a time
when survival wore my name
and softness felt like danger.

But I crossed it—
the space between fear and freedom,
between holding it all in
and letting myself bloom.

Now, I don't ask the wind for permission.
I lean into it—
roots steady,
petals open,
trusting the sun will find me
even in my stillness.

I am no longer the bridge.
I am what grows because I crossed it.
I am the bloom,
unfolding in the quiet.

No longer rushing.
No longer shrinking.
Just being—
in full,
in truth,
in grace.

Mantra
I did not just survive.
I bloomed.
And I'm still blooming.
Ase. 🌿

She was the Thread

She did not ask to be stitched into history—
but still, she showed up in every generation,
pulling herself from silence
like gold from a riverbed.

She was the thread—
not just the story,
but the seam between lifetimes.

The prayer whispered over boiling water.
The kiss placed on a baby's forehead before dawn.
The scream that cracked through every altar of "be quiet."
She was all of it.

And when she finally wrote it down,
the pages didn't just hold poetry—
they held proof
that she lived
wide open.

That she bled beauty.
That she loved without shrinking.
That she unraveled only to reweave herself, stronger.

✦

I am the continuation of every woman who refused to disappear.

✦ I Choose Myself

I didn't wake up brave.
I woke up tired of abandoning myself
for versions of love
that required my silence.

This wasn't a dramatic exit.
No slammed doors.
No final speeches.

Just a quiet moment
where my spirit said,
Enough.

Enough waiting to be chosen.
Enough surviving what I should have been cherished in.
Enough shrinking my needs
to make space for someone else's comfort.

I didn't choose myself
because it was easy.
I chose myself
because staying was costing me my soul.

This choice didn't make me lonely.
It made me honest.
It made me available
for a life that doesn't require self-erasure.

I choose myself
even when it means walking alone for a while.
Even when it means disappointing others.
Even when it means grieving
what I hoped something could become.

This is not selfishness.
This is self-return.

I choose myself
because I am no longer willing
to be the place I disappear.

And with that choice,
the ground began to shift.

SECTION 3- BECOMING — (The Rise)

Becoming is not a destination — it is a
decision made again and again.
Here, the voice steadies.
The fear softens.
The woman begins to trust herself.

These poems live in motion.
They rise mid-breath, mid-choice, mid-leap.

This is where healing turns into embodiment.

This is the moment after the release.
When the ache quiets.
When the body exhales.
When she realizes she is no longer reaching
backward.
Becoming is not sudden.
It is the soft, brave choice to rise anyway.

Becoming

I did not wake up different.
I woke up honest.

Honest about what hurt.
Honest about what I carried too long.
Honest about the love I accepted
when I was starving for safety.

Becoming didn't arrive loudly.
It arrived quietly —
in boundaries,
in pauses,
in the way I no longer abandon myself
to be understood.

I am not finished.
But I am no longer lost.

I am becoming —
and that is enough.

I'm Not Who I Was

I'm not who I was
when survival made my decisions
and staying quiet felt safer than becoming visible.

I'm not who I was
when love required me to disappear,
when rest felt earned instead of deserved,
when my worth waited for permission.

I honored her.
She carried me through.
But she is not the woman writing now.

Something loosened when I stopped asking
who I needed to be
and listened to who I already was.

I felt it in my body first—
the tension releasing,
the breath deepening,
the knowing settling in my bones.

I crossed the threshold
without fireworks,
without applause,
without certainty.

Just truth.

I didn't burn the past down.
I set it down.

I didn't become fearless.
I became honest.

And in that honesty,
I chose myself
not as an ending—
but as a beginning.

This is where becoming starts.

The Woman I Am Learning to Be

She speaks slower now.
Listens deeper.
Moves without explaining herself.

She doesn't chase clarity —
she embodies it.

She trusts her timing.
She rests without guilt.
She knows that alignment
doesn't rush.

Every day,
I meet her a little more.

And every day,
she feels like home.

She Called Her Name Back

She had been named by wounds,
called by labels that were never hers to carry.
Too much. Too soft. Too loud.
Too wild to love right.

But one morning,
she looked in the mirror and whispered,
That is not my name.

She called her name back
from every mouth that spoke it without reverence.
She untangled it from guilt,
washed it in rosewater and salt,
and stitched it to her skin with honey.

She called her name back
until even silence bowed in recognition.
Until the wind pronounced it like prophecy.
Until her spine stood taller under the weight
of her own becoming.

She didn't just reclaim her name—
she redefined it.
And now it rings through generations
like a bell made of thunder and healing.

I speak my name with reverence.
Every time I say it, I return to myself.
I am not who they told me to be—
I am who I choose to remember.

✦

I Am No Longer in a Hurry

I am not late.
I am not behind.
I am not missing anything meant for me.

What's aligned
moves at my pace.

I am learning that rushing
was never intuition —
it was fear.

Now, I let life meet me gently.
I let love recognize me naturally.
I let myself arrive fully
before I invite anything else in.

The Rise

This is not the ending.
This is not the peak.

This is the moment
I stand rooted in who I am becoming
and stop apologizing for the growth.

I rise without force.
Without urgency.
Without fear.

Because I am no longer chasing life.

I am meeting it.

She Was Waiting for Me to Come Back"

for my inner girl, the first golden heart

She used to whisper
to the moon,
wondering when someone
would finally listen
the way she needed.

She braided stars
into silence,
drew maps to safety
in the corners of her dreams.

And I left her—
not out of abandonment,
but survival.
I told her:
"Stay here.
I'll come back when it's safe
to be soft again."

And today,
I did.
With a pen in one hand
and peace in the other,
I met her in a poem
and she said,
"Took you long enough.
Let's go home."

I am safe to return to myself.
My softness is my strength.
I was never lost—only waiting."

★

Why My Name Is Sacred"

(Reflection + poem blend — powerful, ancestral, intimate)

Why My Name Is Sacred

My name was whispered
before I arrived.
Carried through the hands of women
who prayed me into being.

It is the echo of my mother's voice,
the softness of her hope,
the strength of her becoming.
It is the rhythm of every woman
who chose to live,
even when the world tried
to quiet her.

My name is not just letters —
it is lineage.
It is a doorway.
A return.
A remembrance.

It sits on my tongue
like a blessing,
like a promise
I was born to fulfill.

My name is sacred
because I am sacred.
A vessel of prayer.
A keeper of light.
A daughter of women
who survived storms
so I could rise in sun.

When I speak my name,
I speak all of them.
When I honor my name,
I honor every version of me
that needed saving.

My name is a seed.
A legacy.
A home.
A mirror of the woman
I am still becoming.

Mantra: My name carries purpose. My name carries power.

Unfolding

(Neutral Tone)

Not a beginning.
Not an end.
Just the stretch of sky
between what was and what could be.

Not waiting—
but listening.
Not chasing—
but choosing.

A voice rises
not to be heard
but to remember
its own echo.

No names,
no faces—
just the hush of knowing
without needing proof.

Here is the space
where becoming doesn't ask permission.
It just is.

✦ Between What Was & What Will Be

(Bridge)

I didn't heal all at once.
I loosened.
I let go in increments.
I learned that freedom
doesn't arrive loud—
it arrives honest.

There was a moment
after the release
when I didn't know
who I was becoming yet.

I wasn't bound anymore,
but I wasn't risen either.

I was standing in the quiet,
holding both grief and grace,
learning how to breathe
without bracing.

This is where I learned
that rest is not retreat.
That stillness is not failure.
That becoming begins
long before it shows.

I did not rush the next version of me.
I let her form.
I let her listen.
I let her trust the ground beneath her feet.

This space—
between who I was
and who I am becoming—
was holy.

And I honored it.

When the Quiet Loved Me Back
(***channeled, neutral tone)***

It wasn't thunder
that cracked me open—
but the hush
after wanting.

The morning I stopped begging
for the door to swing wide,
it creaked open
on its own.
And light entered
like it knew my name.

No climax.
No grand reveal.
Just a breath that didn't ache
and a mirror that didn't lie.

I met peace
wearing no perfume,
no smile,
no need to perform.

And for the first time,
I was held
without being touched.

I think that's
when the quiet
loved me back.

Right On Time"

She stopped wondering
if she was late,
or early.
She stopped measuring herself
against clocks that were never set
in her favor.

She started listening—
to the rhythm in her ribcage,
the pulse in her palms,
the soft, sacred "now"
that whispered,
"You are exactly where you're meant to be."

Because divine timing
doesn't run on deadlines—
it runs on alignment.
And when it clicks into place,
it doesn't apologize
for how long it took.
It just opens.

Wide.
Warm.
Ready.

I trust the rhythm of my life.
Every unfolding is on purpose.
I arrive exactly when I am meant to.
✦

She Was the Fire and the Pause

for the woman who could say yes, but chose to wait

Her body remembered him—
not just in muscle,
but in memory,
in the ache between thoughts,
in the way silence grew heavy
when he leaned in.

She knew she could have said yes.
Could have let her fire swallow him whole.
But instead,
she kissed him with her energy
and walked away glowing.

Because real power
is knowing you can taste the flame
and still choose to keep it burning
slow.

She wasn't withholding.
She was honoring.

My desire is sacred.
My body is the altar.
And I alone decide when the candle is lit."

★

Reflection: The Leap

There is a sacred power in choosing to show up —
not for a response,
but for the truth of what your spirit feels called to do.

You reached with intention, not expectation.
You let your courage speak in whispers
instead of waiting for the world to shout approval.

This was never about chasing anyone.
It was about listening to spirit —
that subtle nudge,
that undeniable tug in the chest
that says "now."

And now…
you get to let go.
Not in surrender to silence,
but in trust of divine unfolding.

Whatever comes next will meet you with the same energy you sent:
truthful, grounded, whole.

You are magnetic when you're honest.
You are powerful when you choose peace over performance.
And you are already aligned with all that's meant for you.

I release expectation. I honor the voice within.
What's meant for me always knows where to find me.

Soft Power

I used to think power meant endurance.
Holding on.
Pushing through.

But power looks different now.

Power is leaving early.
Power is saying no without apology.
Power is choosing peace
even when chaos is familiar.

I don't need to be loud to be felt.
I don't need to prove to be chosen.

My softness is not weakness.
It is wisdom.

✦ I Am Still Standing

I did not rise by running.
I rose by standing still long enough
to feel the ground remember me.

I stood in my name.
In my breath.
In the bones of the women who came before me
and whispered,
"You are allowed to take up space now."

I stopped chasing versions of myself
that required abandonment.
Stopped calling urgency purpose.
Stopped confusing movement with growth.

Rooted does not mean stuck.
It means supported.

I learned that stability is not the absence of desire —
it is desire with a spine.

I am grounded enough now
to move without losing myself.
Anchored enough
to rise without floating away.

This is how becoming begins:
not from escape,
but from embodiment.

I am still standing.
And because of that —
I am ready to rise.

✦ The Version That Stayed

There was a version of me
who stayed longer than she should have
because leaving felt like failure.

I honor her.
She kept me alive.

But I am no longer her.
I am the woman
who knows when staying
costs more than leaving.

Growth didn't come
when I tried harder —
it came when I chose differently.

She Became the Bridge

for the version of me who loved, birthed, and became.

She used to pray for peace in pieces,
asking the moon to gather her breath
and the sun to burn away the weight.
But motherhood taught her alchemy.
Love taught her presence.
Becoming taught her she was never waiting —
she was remembering.

She is the warmth her daughter reaches for
in midnight's hush.
The softness her partner confesses into.
The fire her ancestors trusted would rise again.
She is both the ache and the answer.
Both womb and word.

And when she stands still,
it's only because Spirit is planting her deeper.
So she can hold the roots,
and birth the revolution.

She became the bridge —
between the girl who didn't know she was enough,
and the woman who knows she is the thread
that stitches futures whole.

I ***am the bridge. I am the root. I am the answered prayer in bloom.***

Section 4 DIVINE LOVE — The Connection

Divine love is not fantasy — it is resonance.
It mirrors truth, not longing.
These poems explore connection without erasure,
intimacy without abandonment, and love that
meets, not chases.

This is love after healing.
Love that listens.
Love that stays awake.

Divine Love (Anchor Poem)

This opens the section.

I no longer ask love to prove itself
through confusion, distance, or pain.
Divine love arrives clear.
It stays.
It chooses.

It does not rush me,
does not fear my depth,
does not ask me to be smaller
so it can feel bigger.

Divine love meets me present,
not potential.
It honors my healing
instead of competing with it.

I am not chasing love.
I am standing where love recognizes me.
And what is divine
always knows where to find me

Love That Knows My Name

He does not study me like a mystery
or approach me like a conquest.
He knows me.

He knows my softness is strength.
My silence is sacred.
My fire is intentional.

He speaks my name
like it belongs in his mouth.
Like he's been practicing.

This love does not forget me
in busy seasons.
It remembers.
It returns.
It remains.

Chosen Without Convincing

I am no longer auditioning
for affection.

I am not explaining my worth
or translating my needs
into something easier to digest.

Divine love chooses me
without convincing,
without delay,
without fear.

It does not hesitate
at my clarity.
It rises to meet it.

The Way You Show Up

Love is not what you promise me
in quiet moments.
Love is how you show up
when life is loud.

You don't disappear
when things get real.
You don't retreat
when emotions deepen.

You stay.
You speak.
You act.

That's how I know
this is love.

Safe Enough to Soften

I soften because I am safe.
Not because I am hoping.

I open because I am met.
Not because I am waiting.

This love does not punish vulnerability.
It protects it.
It does not test my boundaries.
It respects them.

With you,
my nervous system exhales.
My heart rests.
My spirit stays open.

When Love Is Safe

Love does not rush me anymore.
It meets me
where I am standing.

There is no anxiety in its voice.
No confusion in its presence.

Love is not a chase.
It is a recognition.

It does not ask me
to prove my worth
or perform my softness.

It sees me
and stays.

This is the love
that arrives quietly,
steadily,
without spectacle.

And I know it
because my body does not brace.

This Is How I Know (Closing Poem for the Section)

I know because it's peaceful.
I know because I don't overthink.
I know because my body agrees
before my mind does.

I am not anxious.
I am not confused.
I am not waiting.

Love is here.
And it feels like home.

❤️ DIVINE LOVE — The Connection

✦ Love Without Anxiety

I am no longer interested
in love that confuses my nervous system.

I want presence.
Consistency.
A voice that doesn't disappear
when things deepen.

If love arrives,
it will not require
self-betrayal.

It will feel like home —
not a test.

🔥 Divine Love Mantra

Divine Love Mantra

I am not waiting.
I am allowing.

Love meets me
without confusion,
without delay,
without shrinking.

I am chosen in clarity.
I am met in truth.

Ase'.

★

What I Want Is Sacred Too"

for the woman who stopped apologizing for wanting deeply

I want love that remembers me.
Not just in the morning,
but in the space between glances.
In the way his breath slows when I enter the
in the way silence becomes a vow.

I want joy that doesn't flinch.
That laughs loud and ugly
and still gets invited back.

I want peace that stays —
not just visits me after breakdowns.

I want to be chosen in rooms I didn't have to shrink to enter.

I want soft things.
Warm things.
Real things.
I want pleasure without punishment.
Affection without delay.
Presence without performance.

And I no longer make myself smaller
just to make my wanting more palatable.

Because what I want
is sacred.
Not because it's rare —
but because it's mine.
Born of my healing.
Birthed through my becoming.

I don't need to prove I deserve it.
I've already become the version of me who can hold it.
✦ Ase.

I Am Becoming

I am not who I was
and I will never shrink back into her.
I've peeled off layers,
rewritten stories,
and bled poems from every scar.

This is the becoming —
unapologetic,
luminous,
divine.

🌿 She Doesn't Apologize for Her Magic Anymore

for the woman who stopped shrinking to be palatable

She used to dim
because her glow made others squint.
Used to water herself down
like her presence needed softening.

But not anymore.

Now she walks in her fullness.
Unshaken.
Unapologetic.
Unbothered.

Because her power was never the problem—
their comfort was never the goal.

She doesn't explain her intuition.
She doesn't edit her joy.
She doesn't disguise her "yes"
or shrink her "no."

She lets her light burn how it wants to burn.
Wears her crystals like armor.
Keeps her ancestors in her mirror.
And spells protection into every perfume spritz.

She is
woman,
witness,
and wildfire
in one body.

And when they say she's too much—
she smiles.

Because finally,
she is.

She doesn't apologize
for her power anymore.
She just lives in it.
✦ Ase.

Mantra Interlude: Becoming

I no longer shrink for safety.
I bloom for truth.
Even when it's unfamiliar, I rise.
Even when it's quiet, I am heard.

A new version of me is emerging.
Ase'.

🌍 ROOTED — The Ground

(Ancestral + identity integration)

✦ Bloodline, Rest Now

I am the prayer
my lineage whispered
but never spoke aloud.

I rest where they endured.
I love where they survived.
I soften where they hardened
to stay alive.

Bloodline, rest now.
I've got it from here.

(INFINITE — CLOSING ARC)

The Infinite Thread

(Infinite — The Expansion)

Nothing I healed was wasted.
Nothing I lost was random.

Every ending taught me
how to listen deeper.

Every pause refined my timing.

I am no longer afraid
of the unknown —
I am fluent in it.

What's meant for me
is not delayed.
It is aligning.

I am not behind.
I am unfolding.

This thread does not end here.
It widens.

INFINITE — The Expansion

✦ The Infinite Thread

Nothing I lived was wasted.
Nothing I loved was accidental.

Every ending
wove me deeper
into myself.

I am not done becoming.
I am not done loving.
I am not done rising.

This is not the end of the thread —
this is where it extends
beyond what I can see.

Prayer for the Threads Within Me

Let every word I write
be stitched with grace,
braided with truth,
and soaked in remembrance.

May the voices of my grandmothers
rise with mine—
louder than fear,
softer than shame,
brighter than any silence I was ever told to
sit in.

Let my pen be a wand,
my body a temple,
my tears holy water.

I pray for the courage to stay open,
even when I want to fold.
I pray for the strength to remember,
especially what tried to be forgotten.

May this book be an altar—
and every poem,
a candle lit in their name
and mine.

✦

Ase'. And so it is.

🌙 Final Blessing

Final Blessing

May what found you in these pages
remind you of what already lives within you.

May you leave lighter,
truer,
and more willing to choose yourself.

And may every thread
lead you home
to peace.

Ase'.

★

Acknowledgments

To my ancestors—
thank you for the strength I didn't have to earn.

To my daughter—
you are the reason I chose myself.

To every version of me—
thank you for surviving long enough
for me to bloom.

And to you,
reader—
thank you for witnessing this becoming.

ABOUT THE AUTHOR

Cece Hayes is a spiritual life coach, healer, and poet devoted to helping others rise into their highest selves through intentional living, healing practices, and daily empowerment.

Through her work, she inspires others to embrace their authenticity, align with divine purpose, and create lives rooted in gratitude, clarity, and light.

Connect with her:
✨ Instagram: @chayes27_ | @thegirlchat73_
✨ Email: cecehayes88@gmail.com

Thank you for rising with me.

Made in the USA
Coppell, TX
07 July 2026

83663087R00045